EASY PIANO

AUDIO ACCESS INCLUDED

MR. HOFFMAN'S
POPULAR HITS
FOR PIANO

PLAYBACK+
Speed • Pitch • Balance • Loop

To access audio visit:
www.halleonard.com/mylibrary

5004-9012-3694-6779

ISBN 978-1-5400-2581-4

HAL•LEONARD®

Visit Hal Leonard Online at
www.halleonard.com

Contact us:
Hal Leonard
7777 West Bluemound Road
Milwaukee, WI 53213
Email: info@halleonard.com

In Europe, contact:
Hal Leonard Europe Limited
42 Wigmore Street
Marylebone, London, W1U 2RN
Email: info@halleonardeurope.com

In Australia, contact:
Hal Leonard Australia Pty. Ltd.
4 Lentara Court
Cheltenham, Victoria, 3192 Australia
Email: info@halleonard.com.au

TIPS FOR STUDENTS

Listen Before You Learn

You'll learn these arrangements much faster if you listen to the songs before trying to play them. Listen to the original recordings online, and then listen to the online demo tracks included with this book.

 ### Choose Your Level

These arrangements are designed to be flexible according to your skill level. For most songs, I'll give you ideas for how you can adapt each arrangement to be easier or harder. If you're new to piano, start with the Level 1 instructions. Tackle the higher levels only when you feel ready. As you advance in skill, you can always come back later to try the Level 2 or Level 3 challenges.

 ### Super Challenges

Some arrangements have a "Super Challenge" icon. This is an optional challenge designed to help you go even farther with your skills.

Jam with the Backing Tracks

To maximize your fun and excitement when performing, try playing along with the backing tracks provided. Access the tracks online using the code in the front of the book. Listen for the clicks. That's your cue to count off, then start playing. (The number of clicks varies, depending on the time signature and starting beat of the song.)

Rhythm

Since this collection is for beginning pianists, you may expect to find simplified rhythms. In my arrangements, however, I have chosen not to simplify or alter the rhythms from the original. This is because I have found that kids love the excitement of playing the original rhythms, with all their syncopations and complexities.

Can beginner students handle complex, syncopated rhythms? For me, the answer is an emphatic "Yes!" The secret is not to focus on a mathematical, counting approach. Rather, focus on learning the rhythms "by ear," and then use traditional counting only to reinforce and support. If a student listens to a track many, many times, they can internalize complex rhythms, and they will have the great satisfaction of playing it just like the original version.

Online Support

Visit **www.HoffmanAcademy.com** to access video tutorials where I'll guide you through many of these arrangements.

Happy playing!

– Mr. Hoffman

TIPS FOR TEACHERS

Sight-Reading vs. Learning by Ear

Since the goal of this collection is not to teach sight-reading skills, but rather to build a passion for playing the piano, I invite and encourage you to take a more flexible, "by ear" or "by rote" approach for students who are not yet strong sight-readers. The success they find playing these popular titles "by ear" can fuel their motivation for tackling more advanced skills (including sight-reading) in the future.

To help a student learn these arrangements "by ear," encourage them to listen to the track many times on their own at home. Once a student is thoroughly familiar with a piece, they will be able to learn it much more rapidly at the piano. If they are struggling with notes or rhythms, encourage them to sing along as they play (if the piece has lyrics), or listen again to the original track while humming or singing along.

It is also possible to take a hybrid sight/ear approach by asking a student to tackle easier sections using a sight-reading approach, and then guide them through the more difficult sections "by rote."

I hope you enjoy these arrangements with your students as much as I have with mine. Happy music making!

– Joseph Hoffman

CONTENTS

4 LINUS AND LUCY

6 LEAN ON ME

8 FIGHT SONG

10 MISSION: IMPOSSIBLE THEME

12 WHO SAYS

14 REMEMBER ME (LULLABY)

16 HOW FAR I'LL GO

18 WAVIN' FLAG (COCA-COLA® CELEBRATION MIX)

20 SHAKE IT OFF

24 LET IT GO

26 WE WILL ROCK YOU

28 CAN'T STOP THE FEELING!

31 GERONIMO

34 ROAR

38 THIS IS ME

41 COUNTING STARS

44 HE'S A PIRATE

48 About Mr. Hoffman

LINUS AND LUCY

from A CHARLIE BROWN CHRISTMAS

By VINCE GUARALDI
Arranged by Joseph Hoffman

Moderately fast

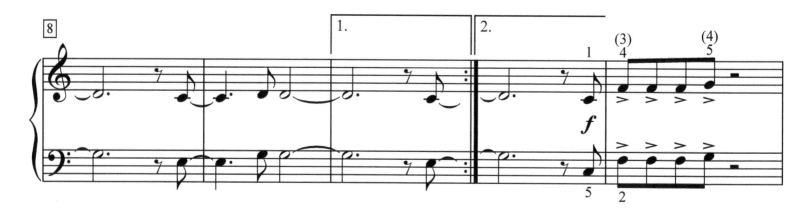

(do a sitting happy dance)

(happy dance time)

(one more happy dance!)

CHOOSE YOUR LEVEL

LEVEL 1: Play right hand only.
LEVEL 2: Play both hands together.

Play along with the online backing track.
Clicks to start: 4

NOTE FOR TEACHERS

Beginner students will likely learn these rhythms most easily "by ear," not by traditional counting methods (1 & 2 &, etc.). Try the following steps to guide a student to succeed:

- Listen to the online demo track several times and have fun humming along.
- Tap the rhythm together while listening to the track.
- At the piano, demonstrate how to play the rhythms correctly and invite the student to imitate.

LEAN ON ME

Words and Music by
BILL WITHERS
Arranged by Joseph Hoffman

Moderately slow, relaxed

al - ways to - mor - row. __ Lean on me. __

mf

CHOOSE YOUR LEVEL

LEVEL 1: Play right hand only.
LEVEL 2: Play both hands together.

MR. HOFFMAN TIP

There are many half notes in this song. Half notes look like this ♩ and are held for two beats. Each time you play a half note in this song, be sure to count two beats out loud or in your mind as you play.

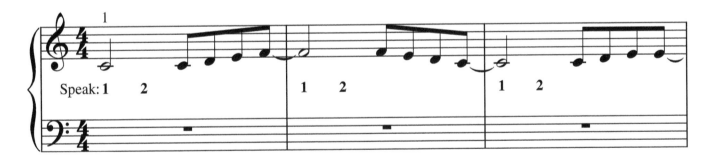

Speak: **1**   **2**   **1**   **2**   **1**   **2**

Play along with the online backing track.
Clicks to start: 4

FIGHT SONG

Words and Music by RACHEL PLATTEN
and DAVE BASSETT
Arranged by Joseph Hoffman

CHOOSE YOUR LEVEL

LEVEL 1: Play right hand only.
LEVEL 2: Play both hands together.

 Play along with the online backing track.
Clicks to start: 3

 SUPER CHALLENGE

Listen to the original recording by Rachel Platten and figure out some of the other sections of the song "by ear." For example, can you figure out which two notes the piano is playing during the song's introduction? (HINT: There's one white key and one black key.)

🍎 **NOTE FOR TEACHERS**

Most rhythms in this song will be learned best "by ear," not by traditional counting methods. Try the following steps to guide a student to succeed at these syncopated rhythms:

- Listen to the original recording by Rachel Platten many times (focus on the chorus) and have fun singing along.
- Try singing along to the online demo track provided with this book.
- At the piano, demonstrate how to play the rhythms correctly and invite the student to imitate. Begin with small chunks.
- Encourage the student to sing along as they play. This can quickly correct many rhythm problems.

MISSION: IMPOSSIBLE THEME

from the Paramount Television Series MISSION: IMPOSSIBLE

By LALO SCHIFRIN
Arranged by Joseph Hoffman

Moderately, with drive

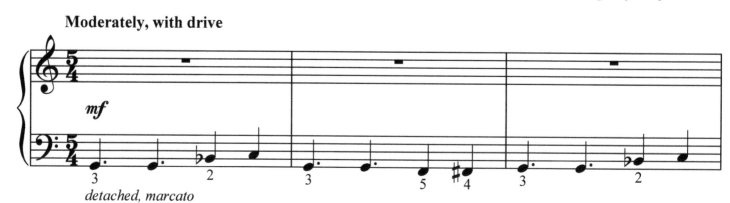

 CHOOSE YOUR LEVEL

LEVEL 1: Skip measures 11–14.
LEVEL 2: Play the entire piece.

MR. HOFFMAN TIP

To master the rhythm of the left-hand part, it can be helpful to count an eighth note pulse.
Remember that:

1 quarter note ♩ = 2 eighth notes ♫

1 dotted quarter note ♩· = 3 eighth notes ♫♪

So, when learning the left-hand part, count "1-2-3" on each dotted quarter note, and "1-2" on each quarter note. Make sure that you keep the pulse steady. A metronome can help: Try setting your metronome between 132–160 bpm (each click is one eighth note).

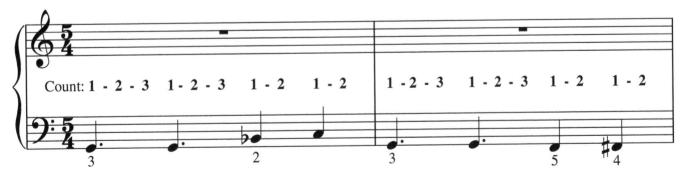

🔊 **Play along with the online backing track.**
Clicks to start: 4

WHO SAYS

Words and Music by PRISCILLA RENEA
and EMANUEL KIRIAKOU
Arranged by Joseph Hoffman

📶 CHOOSE YOUR LEVEL

LEVEL 1: Play right hand only

LEVEL 2: Add chords in the left hand, playing whole notes in each measure as shown below.

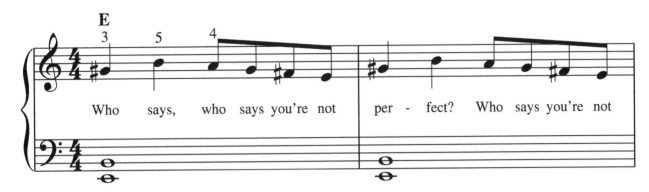

LEVEL 3: Play both hands together as written.

🔊 **Play along with the online backing track.**
Clicks to start: 4

🏆 SUPER CHALLENGE

- Listen to the original recording by Selena Gomez and see if you can play along with the chorus.

- Are there any other sections of the song that you can figure out on the piano yourself? As a hint, here's a short section of the song:

REMEMBER ME
(Lullaby)
from COCO

Words and Music by KRISTEN ANDERSON-LOPEZ
and ROBERT LOPEZ
Arranged by Joseph Hoffman

Tenderly

 MR. HOFFMAN TIPS

- A fermata ⌢ means to pause and hold a note (or rest) for a moment. Can you find and circle all the fermatas in this song? As you play, be sure to take some extra time whenever you come to a fermata.

- This song is meant to be a lullaby. Play it gently, but expressively, like a parent singing to their child.

🔊 **Play along with the online backing track.**
No clicks: guitar plays three notes, pause, then begin playing.

 SUPER CHALLENGE

Add a harmony part in "thirds" in measure 13, as shown below.

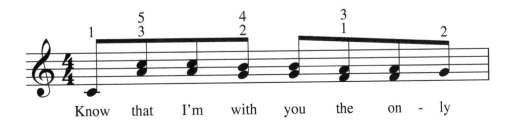

HOW FAR I'LL GO
from MOANA

Music and Lyrics by
LIN-MANUEL MIRANDA
Arranged by Joseph Hoffman

With excitement

See the line where the sky meets the sea? It calls ____

____ me, ____ and no one knows ____

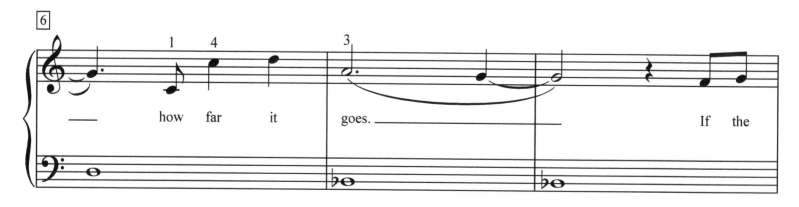

____ how far it goes. ____ If the

wind in my sail on the sea stays be - hind ____ me, ____

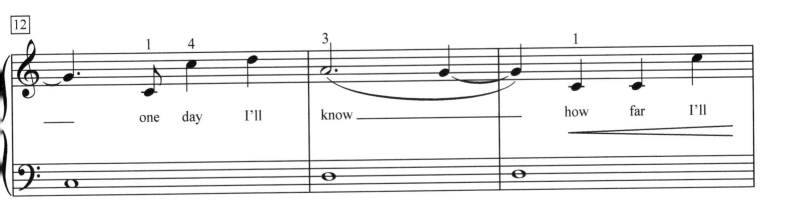

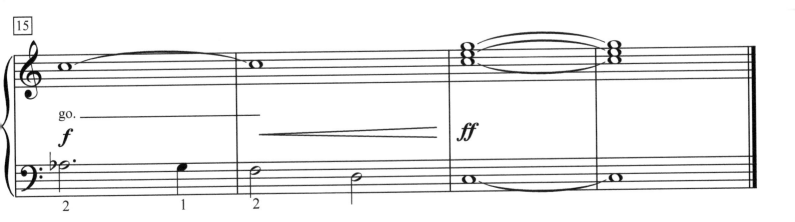

 CHOOSE YOUR LEVEL

LEVEL 1: Play right hand only.
LEVEL 2: Play both hands together.

🔊 **Play along with the online backing track.**
Clicks to start: 3

🏆 **SUPER CHALLENGE**

Make the left-hand part more exciting by replacing all the whole notes with quarter notes in measures 1–14:

WAVIN' FLAG

(Coca-Cola® Celebration Mix)
2010 FIFA WORLD CUP ANTHEM

Words and Music by KEINAN WARSAME,
PHILIP LAWRENCE, BRUNO MARS,
JEAN DAVAL, EDWARD DUNNE
and ANDREW BLOCH
Arranged by Joseph Hoffman

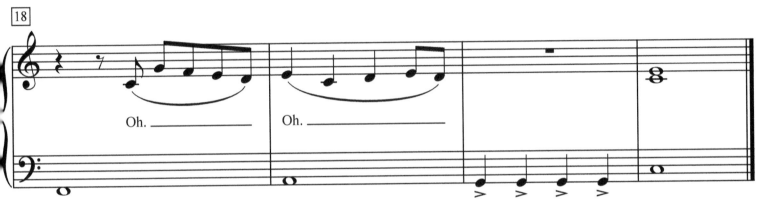

🎵 CHOOSE YOUR LEVEL

LEVEL 1: Play right hand only.
LEVEL 2: Play both hands together.

🔊 **Play along with the online backing track.**
  Clicks to start: 4

🍎 NOTE FOR TEACHERS

For beginner students, the syncopated rhythms in measures 5–8 will be most easily learned "by ear," not by traditional counting methods. Try the following steps to guide a student to succeed at these syncopated rhythms:

- Listen to the original recording by K'naan many times and have fun singing along.
- Try singing along to the online demo track provided with this book.
- At the piano, demonstrate how to play the rhythms correctly and invite the student to imitate.
- Encourage the student to sing along as they play. This can quickly correct many rhythm problems.

SHAKE IT OFF

Words and Music by TAYLOR SWIFT,
MAX MARTIN and SHELLBACK
Arranged by Joseph Hoffman

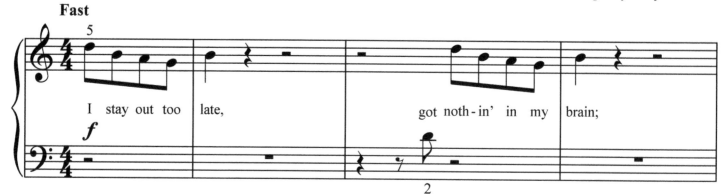

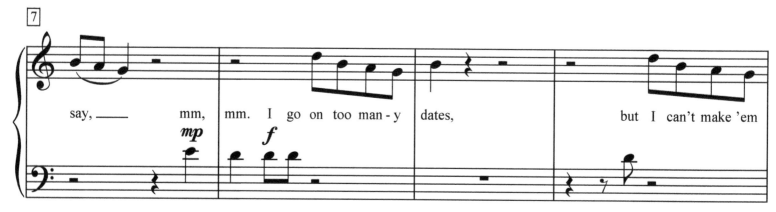

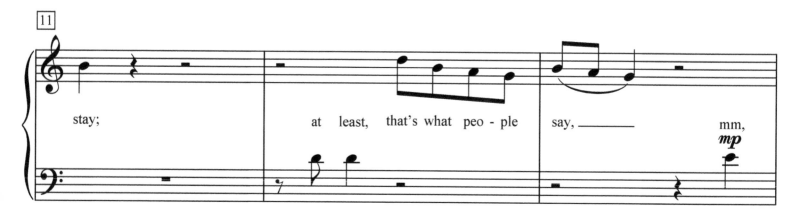

mm. That's what peo - ple say, _____ mm, mm. But I keep cruis - ing,

can't stop, won't stop mov - ing. It's like I got this mu - sic

in my mind say - in', "It's gon - na be al - right." _____ 'Cause the

play - ers gon - na play, play, play, play, play, and the hat - ers gon - na hate, hate,

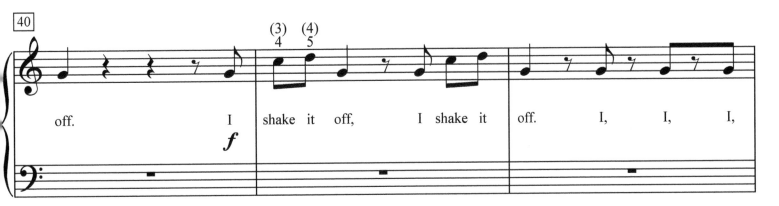

⭐ SUPER CHALLENGE

- Listen to the original recording by Taylor Swift and see if you can play along.
- The original version has additional sections—can you figure out how to play the entire song by ear?

🔊 **Play along with the online backing track.**
Clicks to start: 2

LET IT GO
from FROZEN

Music and Lyrics by KRISTEN ANDERSON-LOPEZ
and ROBERT LOPEZ
Arranged by Joseph Hoffman

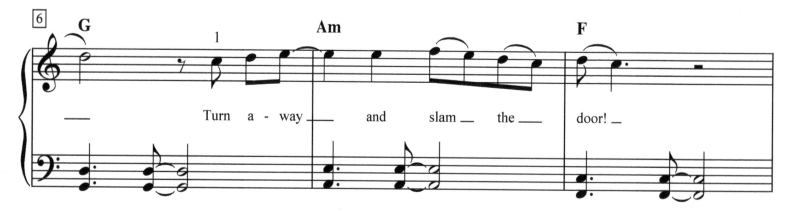

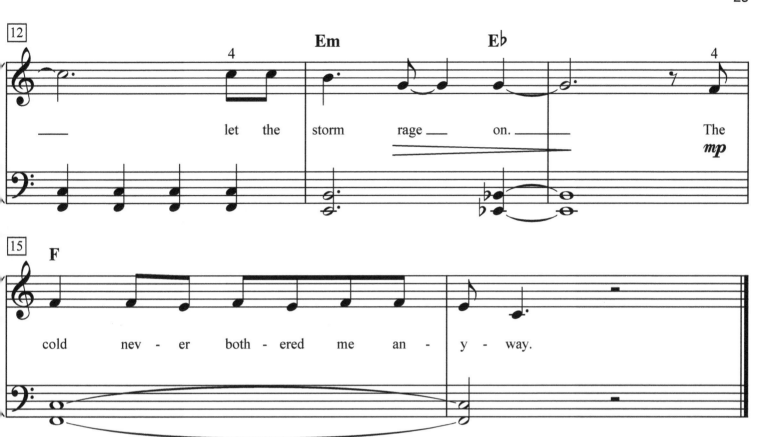

cold nev - er both - ered me an - y - way.

🎵 CHOOSE YOUR LEVEL

LEVEL 1: Play right hand only.

LEVEL 2: Add chords in the left hand, using whole notes for each chord as shown below.

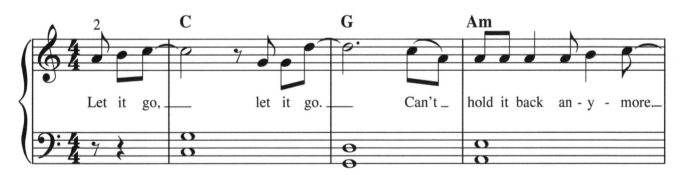

Let it go,___ let it go.___ Can't_ hold it back an - y - more.___

LEVEL 3: Play with both hands together as written.

🔊 **Play along with the online backing track.**
   Clicks to start: 3

WE WILL ROCK YOU

Words and Music by
BRIAN MAY
Arranged by Joseph Hoffman

Steady Rock beat

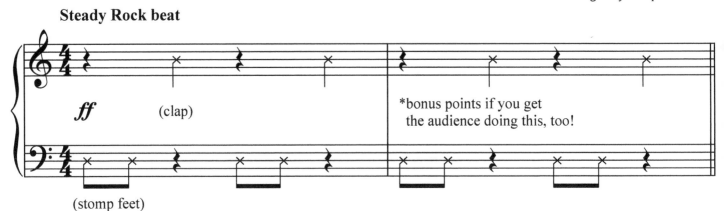

ff (clap)

*bonus points if you get
the audience doing this, too!

(stomp feet)

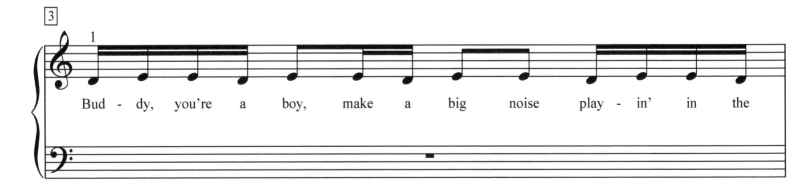

Bud - dy, you're a boy, make a big noise play - in' in the

street. Gon - na be a big man some - day. You got mud on your face, you big dis - grace,

kick - in' your can all o - ver the place. Sing - in' we will, we will

(stomp feet)

 SUPER CHALLENGE

- Listen to the original recording by Queen and see if you can play along.
- Can you figure out how to play the other verses by ear?

🔊 **Play along with the online backing track.**
Clicks to start: 4

🍎 **NOTE FOR TEACHERS**

Most rhythms in this song will be learned best "by ear," not by traditional counting methods. Try the following steps to guide a student to succeed at these syncopated rhythms:

- Help the student become familiar with the melody and rhythm by listening to the original recording by Queen, or the online demo track provided with this book. Have fun singing along.
- At the piano, demonstrate how to play the rhythms correctly and invite the student to imitate. Begin with small chunks.
- Encourage the student to sing along as they play. This can quickly correct many rhythm problems.

CAN'T STOP THE FEELING!

from TROLLS

Words and Music by JUSTIN TIMBERLAKE,
MAX MARTIN and SHELLBACK
Arranged by Joseph Hoffman

CHOOSE YOUR LEVEL

LEVEL 1: In measures 1–7, skip all eighth notes and sixteenth notes, and just play "dance, dance, dance." From measure 8 to the end, play only the right hand. (Play along with the online backing track for the most fun!)

LEVEL 2: Same as Level 1, but now add the left-hand part from measure 8 to the end.

LEVEL 3: Add all the fast eighth notes and sixteenth notes in measures 1–7, so now you're playing the full version from start to finish.

🔊)) **Play along with the online backing track.**
Clicks to start: 4

NOTE FOR TEACHERS

Most rhythms in this song will be learned best "by ear," not by traditional counting methods. Try the following steps to guide a student to succeed at these syncopated rhythms:

- Help the student to become familiar with the melody and rhythm by listening to the original recording by Justin Timberlake. Have fun singing along.
- Try singing along to the online demo track provided with this book.
- At the piano, demonstrate how to play the rhythms correctly and invite the student to imitate. Begin with small chunks.
- Encourage the student to sing along as they play. This can quickly correct many rhythm problems.

GERONIMO

Words and Music by GEORGE JOSEF SHEPPARD,
AMY LOUISE SHEPPARD and JASON BOVINO
Arranged by Joseph Hoffman

Say, Ge - ron - i - mo! Say, Ge - ron - i - mo! Say, Ge - ron - i - mo!

Say, Ge - ron - i - mo! Say, Ge - ron - i - mo! Can you *mf legato*

4

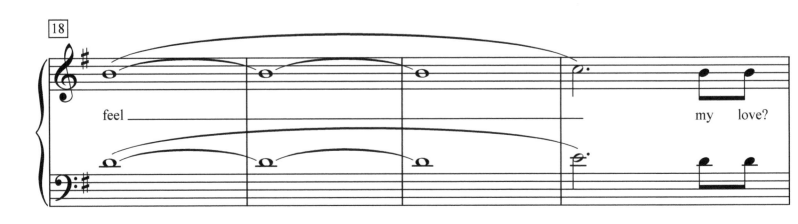

feel _____ my love?

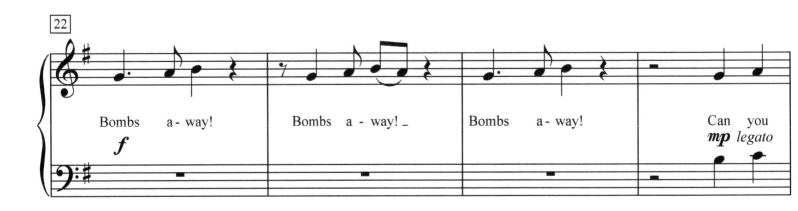

Bombs a - way! *f* Bombs a - way! _ Bombs a - way! Can you *mp legato*

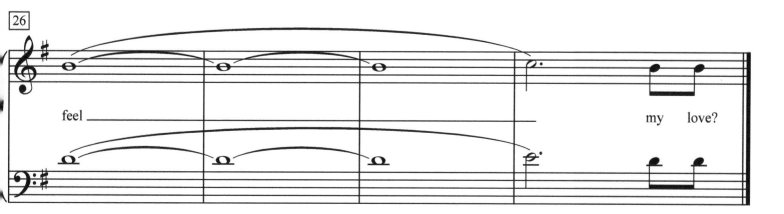

feel _____ my love?

 MR. HOFFMAN TIPS

- To stay in sync with the backing track, remember to count the beats during the longer rests. Counting is how you'll know exactly when to start playing again.

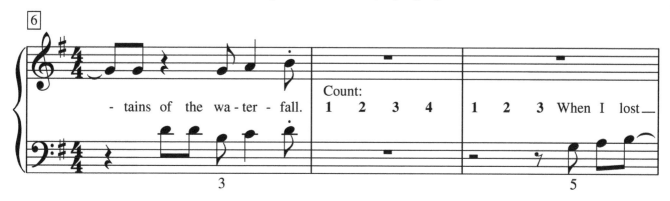

- tains of the wa-ter-fall. Count: 1 2 3 4 | 1 2 3 When I lost __

- It's also very important to count while you are holding the long, tied whole notes. Remember: Great musicians are always counting!

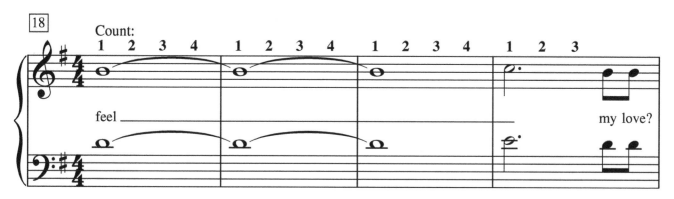

Count: 1 2 3 4 | 1 2 3 4 | 1 2 3 4 | 1 2 3

feel _____ my love?

🔊 **Play along with the online backing track.**
Clicks to start: 3

ROAR

Words and Music by KATY PERRY,
MAX MARTIN, DR. LUKE,
BONNIE McKEE and HENRY WALTER
Arranged by Joseph Hoffman

Moderate Pop Shuffle

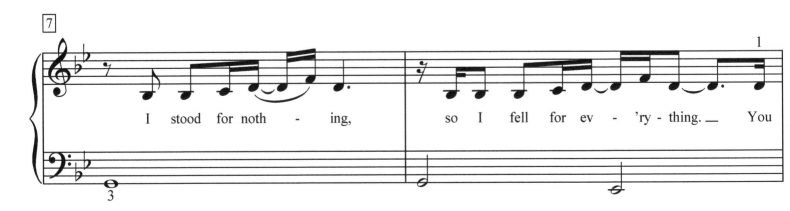

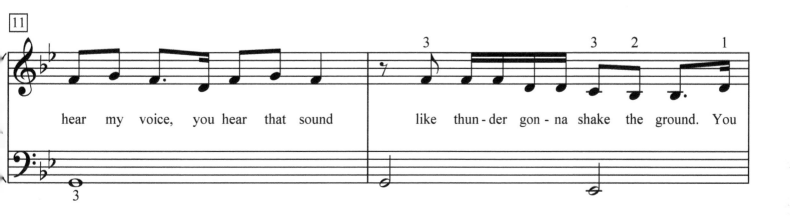

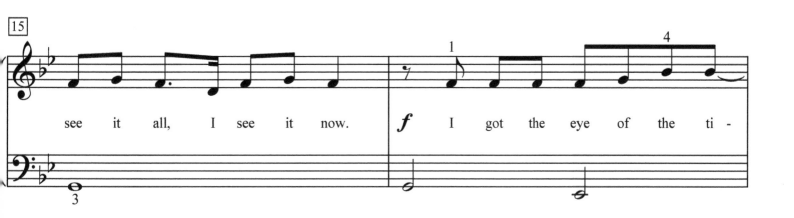

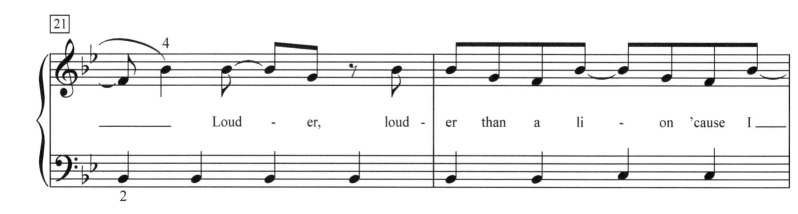

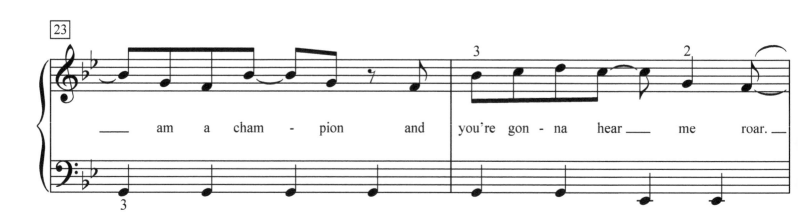

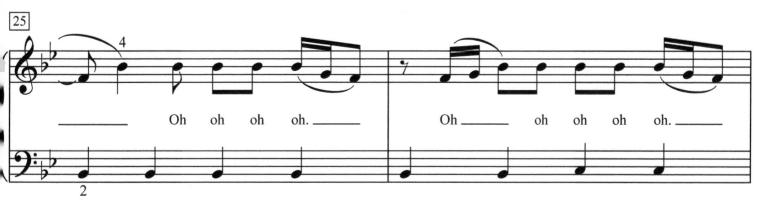

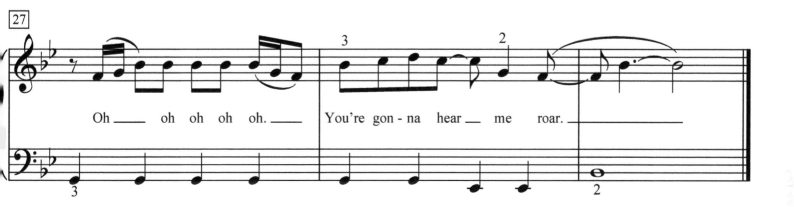

 ## CHOOSE YOUR LEVEL

LEVEL 1: Play the chorus (measure 16 to the end), right hand only.

LEVEL 2: Play the entire song, right hand only.

LEVEL 3: Play the entire song, hands together.

🔊 **Play along with the online backing track.**
Clicks to start: 4

🏆 **SUPER CHALLENGE**

- Listen to the original recording by Katy Perry and see if you can play along.

- Can you figure out how to play any other sections of the song by ear?

THIS IS ME
from THE GREATEST SHOWMAN

Words and Music by BENJ PASEK
and JUSTIN PAUL
Arranged by Joseph Hoffman

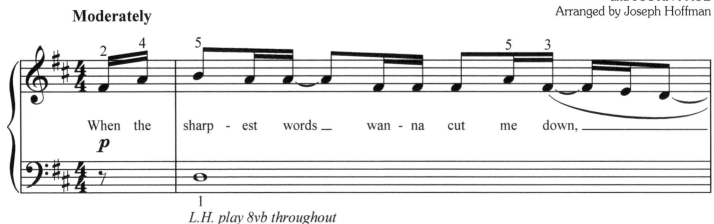

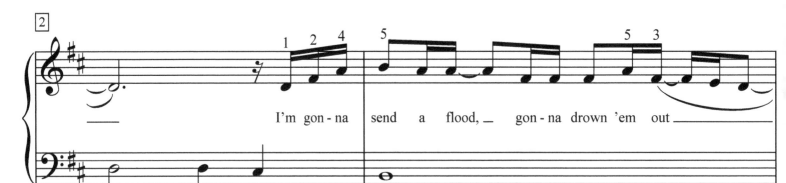

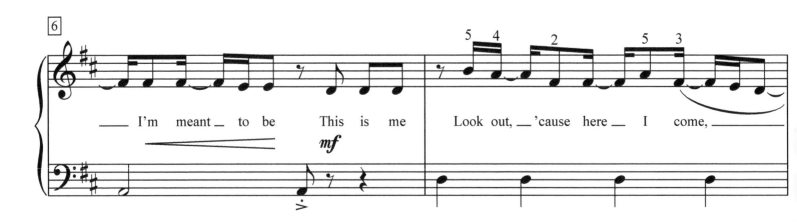

and I'm march - in' on ___ to the beat ___ I drum ___

I'm not scared ___ to be seen ___ I make no ___

___ a - pol - o - gies   This is me   (Oh ___

f

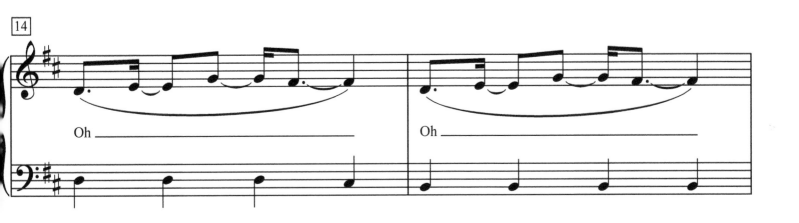

Oh ___   Oh ___

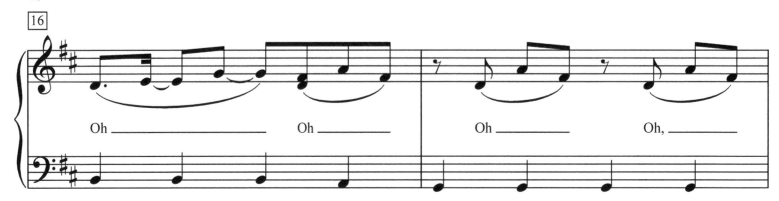

Oh _____ Oh _____ Oh _____ Oh, _____

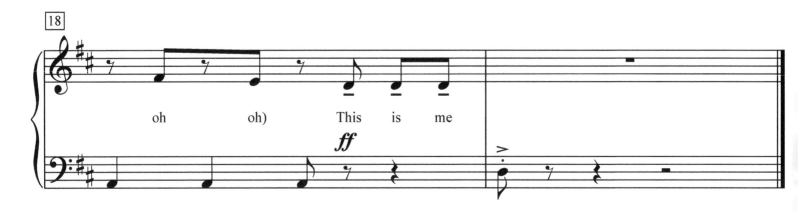

oh oh) This is me

ff

 CHOOSE YOUR LEVEL

LEVEL 1: Play right hand only.
LEVEL 2: Play both hands together.

🔊 **Play along with the online backing track.**
Clicks to start: 4

🏆 **SUPER CHALLENGE**

- Listen to the original recording from *The Greatest Showman* and see if you can play along.
- Can you figure out how to play any other sections of the song by ear?

COUNTING STARS

Words and Music by
RYAN TEDDER
Arranged by Joseph Hoffman

Late - ly I been, I been los - in' sleep, _

dream - in' a - bout _ the things that we could be. But, ba - by, I been,

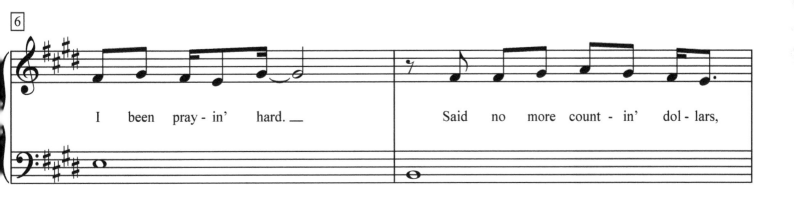

I been pray - in' hard. _ Said no more count - in' dol - lars,

we'll be count - in' stars, _____ yeah, we'll be count - in' _____ stars. _

Faster; Pop-Rock dance groove

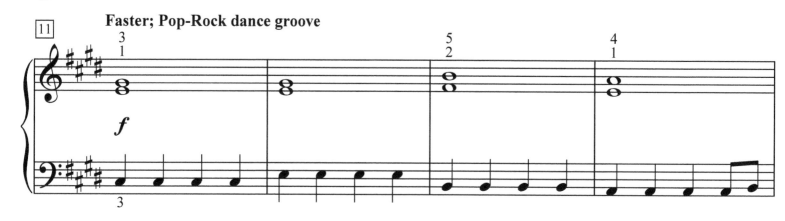

Late - ly I been, I been los - in' sleep, __ dream - in' a - bout __ the things that

we could be. But, ba - by, I been, I been pray - in' hard. __

CHOOSE YOUR LEVEL

LEVEL 1: Play only the first page and end at the fermata.
LEVEL 2: Play the entire song.

Play along with the online backing track.
Clicks to start: 4

NOTE FOR TEACHERS

Most rhythms in this song will be learned best "by ear," not by traditional counting methods. Try the following steps:

- Help the student become familiar with the melody and rhythm by listening to the original recording by OneRepublic, or the online demo track provided with this book. Have fun singing along.

- At the piano, demonstrate how to play the rhythms correctly and invite the student to imitate. Begin with small chunks.

- Encourage the student to sing along as they play. This can quickly correct many rhythm problems.

HE'S A PIRATE

from PIRATES OF THE CARIBBEAN: THE CURSE OF THE BLACK PEARL

Written by HANS ZIMMER,
KLAUS BADELT and GEOFF ZANELLI
Arranged by Joseph Hoffman

Fast, with excitement

L.H. play 8vb throughout

 MR. HOFFMAN TIPS

- To master the rhythm of this theme, it's important to start very slowly and count the beat. Since we are in 6/8 meter, each eighth note will equal one beat.

  ♪ = 1 beat   ♩ = 2 beats   ♩. = 3 beats

- Write in the six counts for each measure, as shown below.

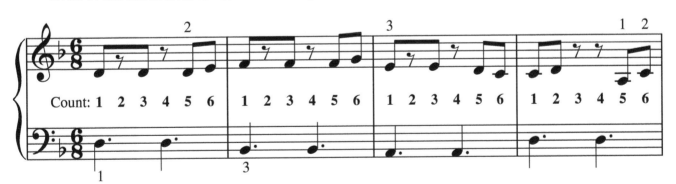

- While practicing, try using a metronome to keep a steady pulse. At first, play very slowly, with the metronome set to between 88–112 bpm (each click equals one eighth note). When you can play confidently, without pausing, gradually increase the speed.

🔊 **Play along with the online backing track.**

Clicks to start: 4 (one click = ♩.)

ABOUT MR. HOFFMAN

JOSEPH HOFFMAN began playing the piano at age six. In high school, he studied with Alfred Mouledous, principal pianist for the Dallas Symphony Orchestra. While continuing his musical studies in piano and conducting at Brigham Young University, Mr. Hoffman was appointed chorusmaster and conductor for numerous BYU opera productions, including *Carmen* and *The Pirates of Penzance*. He conducted the 300-voice University Chorale and taught courses for music majors in music theory, conducting and sight-singing.

To help pay his way through graduate school, Mr. Hoffman began teaching piano lessons to kids in the neighborhood. He wanted his students to love music and playing the piano, but he struggled to find a piano method that provided a well-rounded musical training, while still being fun and engaging. Over the next several years, he made it his personal quest to study all he could about learning theory, and he actively researched the best methods available for teaching music. It was from these years of study, exploration, and experimentation that the "Hoffman Method" of teaching piano was born.

After graduating with a Master of Music in 2005, Mr. Hoffman was appointed as faculty in BYU's School of Music, where he taught music theory and conducting for two years. In 2007, Mr. Hoffman decided to pursue a lifelong dream and moved to Portland, Oregon with his wife and two sons to start a music academy. Hoffman Academy of Music – Portland now serves over 250 local students with a faculty of 12 teachers.

Mr. Hoffman is also an active composer and conductor, and his original works have been heard in many performance halls. From 2011–2013, he served as orchestra conductor of the Portland Ensign Choir and Orchestra.

Mr. Hoffman regularly serves as an adjudicator of piano festivals and events, and provides training to other piano teachers on the "Hoffman Method." His most recent project is to share the Hoffman Method with the world by creating a series of video piano lessons and online learning games on his website **HoffmanAcademy.com**. Mr. Hoffman is thrilled to now be sharing his passion for music and piano with thousands of kids and adults around the world!